Joyce Shintani

WORDS I COULDN'T STOP

Collection curated by James Laval

Cover design by Christian Bär
www.lektorat-baer.de

Designs courtesy of
Tatiana Vásquez Arellano
www.holamiraestudio.cl

Publication by Lektorat Bär
www.lektorat-baer.de, Stuttgart, Germany

Herstellung und Verlag:
BoD – Books on Demand
Norderstedt, Germany

ISBN 9783753496863

Words I Couldn't Stop

Joyce Shintani

Poems

Volume 1

1983 – 1990

1 Innocence

Attending

Shadow thing lurks inside
robbing breath and time;
    makes spring thrush envied sister,
    whispers stabs at night.

What hard thing beneath the breast?
cramping, sparking mine!
    Tight crumpled knot–
    whole galaxy–
    waits to feel
    unfurled.

Childhood

Lacerated innocence
black-boxed in pain
desperation insensate—
numbness the only surcease
from metal-toothed horror.

2   Flush of Life

Fifth Month in Germany

Skirt: crisp cotton
desert-hot air
and asphalt
Santana on open face
open belief, I can do it;
possibility—a probability.
Shiny auto new
clean and hot
glinting expectations.
Steel, concrete, hope—
all of a package.
Face to sun
bright smile unafraid—
    unaware:
        emptiness behind openness.

Cloud gray day
Regenschnee
lead-air pressure
Hölderlin-heavy immobility
    stasis—
    fixed on
    vorbei.

Oh, California
Oh, young half-woman…

Birthday

I view the hurdles I must take
    to pass from girl to wife,
yet cling to toys and high-pitched voice,
    elude responsibility.

But a humming tone reminds me:
    I'm bound to stretch
    if I'll catch
    my thirty-second year.

Homage to Barbara

Small compact form
white satin skin
boar bristle hair.
Softness, comfort, balsam.
Prickly warrior for truth!

Beside you
I marvel
at your pillowy grace
and want to leash you in.

You bark then a word
—independent flight!
The ouch:
hugging tight
let go.

That Fellow

That fellow
who makes
the popping noise
with his mouth
as he passes–
it seems he's just
nothing–
better–
to do
or pop
or think.

Tram Stop

Summer's becoming–
warm and bursting;
streetcar, sweats.
Young men bored,
punked hair, dirty denims.
My hand cold on the rail.
Young men debarking,
one leans on the rail–
his arm's hot.

Off streetcar, change station,
escalator, corridor, stairs,
faces, bodies, and then
a man
in fine gray shirt
and fine black pants
with fine silver glasses
and combed hair.
Stands, tight,
not looking, looks.
One, two, three times,
back and forth and back.
I study his looking.
His body tilts,
no longer easily erect.

To stand strong alone
is no easier for him.

Game

I shorten tiresome
late train home
with expectancy
of telephone.

Distract myself with
playful things–
what word will answer he
my ring!

Visit

There's your knock at door and heart,
dark you fill my threshold.

Shy, distressed, from town you come
wafting wine and weary.

Querulous you start, then quick
you slip beneath the cover:

nervous flutter, fast on skin,
doubtful seeking other–

calmer, deep we draw us in,
night becomes our eider.

Hard, distracted, open–you–
fill me overflowing.

Unison

My solo torch
    gleams low at night;
    real fire burns inside.

In you—sparks wild!—
    flame of delight
    is sated, then, dim.

Fire scintillates
    but sparks alone
    can't fuel
    true Eros' beam.

Source

The special wound I have
    doesn't bleed,
    it weeps
tears, refined from
    mountain streams—
    biting running song.

Winter: crystal,
    frozen dew,
    in warmer glow a blush.
In Spring: a spray,
    a flush of life;
    Autumn: dry and brush.

Wound companion,
    bosom friend,
    we live as one, we two.
I dress it and caress it, yet—
    it will not heal,
    it keeps.

3 Eruption

Dry in a Storm

I see a storm
    from far away,
I see its drops
    distinctly;
I'm cut with rain,
    and aching wet,
yet swim in tearless sea.

I know the storm
    that breaks a limb,
I know the crack-
    ing split.

But here, now mute,
    is fury's rage,
and dry is what's
    within.

Rose

Rose, your violet stuns,
and heavy is my head
from perfume
wafting from your glow.

Gentle petals
could whisper a cloud
on my dry cheek.

Rose—spread slow your soft secrets
that I might spy heaven
in your indigo.

Odors

A body's smells:
ceaseless surprises
from impertinent places
at inopportune moments.

Refreshing confusion:
is the pungency
grime–
or sublime?

Scents

Of fragrances I could have given
    when I a girl was still
I less possess, for older now,
    I many blossoms gave.

Bouquet I have
    —if it's delight—
I offer you,
breathe deep.

But need you not,
    before I'm burden
    rather I'd recede.

Young Blond Poet

Oft an inner landscape's rough,
overgrown with underbrush–
or garbaged.

Your voice breathes at dizzy heights
Air thin–
cutting, clean.

Cloudless days we,
intimately,
graze upon horizons.

Dinner Conversation

It wasn't right, it didn't do—
    I broke decorum's rule!
I blundered in and lived—a truth—
    where eloquence was due.

In clogs I trod fine parquetry
    whose gleam was wit and brain;
a humble word I blurted out
    then watched it writhe and ooze.

Embarrassment you tried to soothe,
    I played the game and cooed.
Behind my nodding mask I hid—
    no one saw the blood.

GK

I'd always slept shallow
    in my slender white cot
    till I came for a visit to you.

Like hands full of poppies
    you cupped me up tender
    strong arms on great chest
    held my head.

Hard lips and dry eyes
    sandy brush on my face–
    the light wisp of your kiss
    surprised.

Floration

I finally—
         touched you!
Orchestration of
devastation
exhortation of the bowels!
Pounding implosion,
rhythmic
highwire
screech;
throbbing, glowing,
flooding, flowing;
blood-red
opening
liquid lips;
covered in
pulsating,
exploding,
germinating
transformation;
transcending
woven-dream webs;
correlation,
unification warmth
wrapped in
over-under;
eruption,
circulation,

inhalation,
feeling:
webbed palms warm,
winsome whine,
gurgling coo,
liquid low,
skin–electricate–

all this–
from a kiss!

Lover,

If I'd your tender throat right now
between my muscled hands,
I'd do like the farmer-Frau,
efficient and without emotion—
a sharp firm twist—
make short work of you,
silly, conceited rooster.

Maybe I'd rather
squeeze you out slow,
till blood and gold
ran like fat.
I'd collect them then
and pay your creditors—
so your wife could live
in peace.

Mouthful

I am a mouth
    that eats a man
    and later spits the pit.

I've gorged on life
    but still not sated
    would bite into
    tongue-singeing diamonds.

Account

Eye
wrinkles–
close to kiss
wrinkles so crinkly
I'd hold them,
fold them,
find them;
suddenly soft
I see your
naked ache
swell to meet our balm.
    Gaping hole,
    this black scare,
    endless
    wordless
    night.
Eyes brown
eyes dark
brown eyes
my eyes
many wrinkles
simple wrinkles
gentle wrinkles to miss
near
    far
    Nearness–
    weirdness

hole–
my likeness refusing,
words ignoring–
ramping lust
thrust absently
upon me.
    Far, far a past,
    fast past to fear–
    blackness,
    a vacuum
    so complex
    no relax.

I bade you, sincere,
"Go."

Riposte

Dumpf
wie Schwarz,
Echolos
wie Dichtfilz
ist Deine
Leidenschaft,
Michael.

Sparrow

Beast stalks
animal paces
smells the hunt
feels its prey
in jungle mate is near—
I could spring downstairs
and catch a bird…

In my soft-speaking cove
bite off its head
crack its skull and feel
hot blood
swell,
pump,
thick and salt
into my waiting
fleshless
mouth.

Adamant I pace
burning my cage
windows barred,
ironed, and exitless.
I smell—
smoldering I sniff
the needed scent
knowing you're near

in the city
and rain and work and
Belief
won't tame…

What would I wish!
　　soft hair, pouting flesh
　　"Plow in deeply, cultivate!
　　Plant something hard that grows,"
　　the arid flanks insist,
but knowing: fulfillment's in–
refraining.

The rain is lush–
in pouring, bathes;
it suits me now,
my gush.

Out there's the culprit,
force unseen
hidden silvery beams;
past rain and blanket sky
is the wanton villain.
Her magic light smile
her hard bright eyes
struck me
sparked me
pricked me alight–
The moon's at fault!

relentless, merciless driver
and you can't drown it, rain,
with your dull, deafening crescendo;
flames just jump,
leap higher
in tandem harmony
in vibration
correlation
trill, clean queen!
Abstract union granted me.

But mock me rain—don't.
Here my brow, touch me;
burning, soothe.
Come, soak Moan's ceaseless cycle,
damp and dilute
lax her steel
magnetic guys'
autocracy.
Loose my bonds,
ligaments let limp,
cool, slacken, slake;
decontract, dampen, dangelate,
let limp limbs swingle, sway.
Heartless moon,
coercive tyrant
with your crack whip slit—
Abdicate!
let me breathe,

release these muscles
free.
Pound down, dear rain,
wash and flood,
flush out Nature's decree;
abduct me,
eradicate,
take far away.

Come, sweet sleep,
let's elope
to dream eternity.

4 Fire Heart's Stones to Stars

Face of Joy

Wordless green Anger
wells in gall from bottomless
pools of shut-up swallowed
hurts.
If I'd your face
between my fingers
I'd rub your mug in the
eye-stinging green
till you
choke and repent and scream howl.

Trickling and squirting,
bilious hot liquid
spurts out from festers inside—
source quite different but
poison as potent
as the brown-black paste
sweated
from my sex wounds.

Motivation

What sun burned
when first I sensed
the secreted calyx
of guilt?

By what lust bitten
did I excited penetrate
her gorging chest
of urges,

discovering spurs that—
pricking my flanks—
made me writhe
in action?

Ambition burned
to decorate myself,
to make something glitter
for my audience.

A cloud blooded the sky
the day I tender reached
trembling
for her needles.

Révérence

Whence this shield
    that strong as steel
    can wither like a bloom?

Who gave man love
    to burn his mouth
    or fire heart's stones
    to stars?

5   Urgency Is Authority

Sacramental

I lived in a dusk,
not morning or night—
vast breathingless, senseless void.

After years in the dark
I received greatest Gift:
the shimmering Light of the Word;

but alone in the Word
I grew to the need
of a sky to count the stars in.

Long, long, long
and slow, like a mist,
the hint of your sunrise tinged my
horizon:

A lightening grey,
muted velvet dawn
that seeped to a violet hue,

then, luxuriant,
spread to more than the eyes—
I felt warm by this sun, and I knew

that these rays–
my rare golden comfort–
would shine in the bitterest storm.

Unspeakable grace:
the privilege of eyes,
a cry in the shade to define;

to give you Breath
and take from you mine,
I need to sing through the Winter.

Endowment of joy,
soft union, content–
bounty of heart is divine.

Unwed

In taking less
I choose the more,
for–
perfume I would own,
could,
through custom,
lose its burst–
of which I am
possessed.

Euterpe's Counsel

Leave the trunk,
reach for topmost spray—
be thus near
fullest heaven!

Perilous Practice

The simpler knack
    is learn the trick
    to coax a thought without;
though choosing ideas
    is the *art*
for thoughts lie all about.

Anonymous

A Portuguese
without a name
polishes weekly
the escalator,

with devotion to sparkle
incongruous
with insult
that is the job.

Who ever stops
to celebrate
how he works
and how he dies?

A puzzled brow,
or lugging hand,
or that Infinite Tracking
Eye?

Patience

Living presents such
    smarting dilemmas—
wince prompts search
    for remedy.

But most conundrums
    haven't 'yes' or 'no',
but only 'black' or 'wait'
    as reply.

Palimpsest

A wisp of cloud
took away tonight
the tears I'd saved
for you.

A calm memory—
lisping outward
bound to solid inward—
caresses the ache
and sweetens necessity
of detachment—
soft detachment,
like a stroke of caring
that parts.

But warm remains
what does not fade:
the sharing I knew
with you.

Deference

I flaunt myself
without permit
of conscience's decree,

for isolation's
bruising pinches
overrule—

Urgency is
Authority.

6 Final Closure

Afternoon

The field is mowed,
only the stubble
and grasshoppers
remain.
The sun's long rays
still warm the skin
but from behind
the air is cooling.

The hazing shine speaks release,
the ripened fruit is gathered.
Soon the chill,
the short, grey days
will force us all
to other fires.

New Food

Today I caught
    after years and years
    of searching earnestly
A glimpse of me
    as others see,
    an answer to the riddle.

I'm like a fly,
    or worse,
I observe–
    my chief nutrition.

I live like the leech
from blood.

Split Vision

This old hag,
unwanted visitor,
sits in my room
making her own conversation.

She's older now,
lost her flush,
and drying wrinkles emphasize
her cosmetic.

The glow that once burnished her eye
is gone
and the selfishness of her musings
is naked.

I once thought her worthy,
a dame to revere;
I gave her my attention
and even imitation.

Now I see her differently
sitting here in my chair—
animated
and smoking cigarettes
with my lipstick on her mouth.

Waiting

To test the sweet
of your blush
lies in me
like the tsunami,
century wave,
born of earth's shudder
unseen on ocean floor,
washing and waving
taking and driving,
possessing in its thrall
land, manimal–all.

So rises and pushes
this other shudder
welling from its molten core,
swelling and willing to break–
boundless spraying veil!–
on a chest:
    white beach pliant,
on a cheek:
    soft whispering dune,
over mouth:
    brilliant vermillion
    ember of morning–
    my sun.

Dissolving

In still hours
when no eye perceives,
the matter of the world's
slowly decomposing.

In atom ticks
the universe clock
creeps toward
its final undoing,

and every blip,
cosmic drop,
carries one of us
closer
to the soundless zero vacuum.

Raiders

I have voracious boots–
busy, silent moles that
gnaw all day on my stockings
till the stuffing's down limp
around the knees.

A second unseen nibbler,
blinded eye and
stub webbed paw,
strips the vital roots
of psyche's tree,
sucking out juices
invisibly.

Flash

In the long slanting light
of late summer
that shone on full grain
and fat on my back,

I saw the length of endlessness,
the measure of eternal mile
and, looking again, saw
how short
that trudge is.

Foreshadow

I hear a call–
the aunt of love
is heading home.
A void sucks my heart–
cleft so great
the mind balks…

My mirror talks:
Your young eye's clouded.
One day the black
will suck you out too–
you'll have been.

Clouded eye sights slipping refraction
grasps–
glimpse
of final closure.

Function

Pound of
dead flesh
under sighs
makes diamonds:
    disembodied,
    odorant—
    creation.

Who'd crush coals,
instead—
presses gems
in my cold bedrock.

Vocation

Mine to feel the leaves on trees
and measure how blue the sky.

Mine it is to count the tears
the world forgot to cry.

Goal

Stones
under feet
suck blood
for the earth.

Rose
of your cheek
is red,
my one.

Inevitability

Damnable paradox:
young woman shy
educated aptly
loses simplicity.

Melos

Distant milk,
scalding,
sweetens
acid night
moments.

Beyond
wait
stars.

On My Chest Milk Sours

More than
the whiteness of your chest
I value
its future.
I'd lay my cheek
and, steadied, with you
stride through the years.

There we hope to breathe
our childhood dreams.

With time, we felt them passing,
and I heard you gasp.
Time soured the milk on my chest,
and your eye failed.

North winds bleached hope
from my rainbow.
Art imitated nature's panoply,
and transparent arches deflected
detection.

But after the future
comes a clear spread of blue.
And we'll breathe again
the hope that
we as children dreamed.

Index